Doing Business Ethically

The Lessons Learned Series

Learn how the most accomplished leaders from around the globe have tackled their toughest challenges in the Harvard Business Press *Lessons Learned* series.

Concise and engaging, each volume in this series offers fourteen insightful essays by top leaders in industry, the public sector, and academia on the most pressing issues they've faced. The *Lessons Learned* series also offers all of the lessons in their original video format, free bonus videos, and other exclusive features on the 50 Lessons companion Web site **www.50lessons.com/ethics**.

Both in print and online, *Lessons Learned* contributors share surprisingly personal and insightful anecdotes and offer authoritative and practical advice drawn from their years of hard-won experience.

A crucial resource for today's busy executive, *Lessons Learned* gives you instant access to the wisdom and expertise of the world's most talented leaders.

Other books in the series:

Doing Business Ethically

LES50NS

www.50lessons.com/ethics

Boston, Massachusetts

Printed in the United States of America
14 13 12 11 10   5 4 3 2 1

Library of Congress Cataloging-in-Publication Data

Doing business ethically.
        p. cm. — (Lessons learned)
    Includes bibliographical references and index.
    ISBN 978-1-4221-3985-1 (pbk. : alk. paper)
  1. Business ethics. I. Harvard Business School. Press.
    HF5387.D638 2009
    174'.4—dc22

                                        2009034988

In partnership with 50 Lessons, a leading
provider of digital media content, Harvard
Business Press is pleased to offer *Lessons
Learned*, a book series that showcases the
trusted voices of the world's most experi-
enced leaders. Through personal story-
telling, each book in this series presents the
accumulated wisdom of some of the world's
best-known experts and offers insights into
how these individuals think, approach
new challenges, and use hard-won lessons
from experience to shape their leadership
philosophies. Organized thematically
according to the topics at the top of managers' agendas—leadership, change management, entrepreneurship, innovation, and
strategy, to name a few—each book draws
from 50 Lessons' extensive video library of
interviews with CEOs and other thought
leaders. Here, the world's leading senior

A Note from the Publisher

executives, academics, and business thinkers speak directly and candidly about their triumphs and defeats. Taken together, these powerful stories offer the advice you'll need to take on tomorrow's challenges.

As you read this book, we encourage you to visit **www.50lessons.com/ethics** to view videos of these lessons as well as additional bonus material on this topic. You'll find not only new ways of looking at the world, but also the tried-and-true advice you need to illuminate the path forward.

⇥ CONTENTS ⇤

Contents

Doing Business Ethically

Examining the Definition of Right and Wrong

Truett Tate

Group Executive Director, Lloyds TSB

LLOYD'S TSB HAS become a long-term partner with Opportunity International, a nonprofit microfinance organization with a very interesting and different concept. It actually creates banks in the emerging

Doing Business Ethically

markets that make microfinance loans. We identify very heavily with the group because it is entrepreneurialism in its most incipient state. The average loan is £80. It has a particular bias toward women because its own research indicates that in many emerging economies, the women are more responsible, have a stronger sense of family, and have a better repayment track record. But I digress to a certain degree. That's to give you a little sense of Opportunity International.

The question of ethics comes in as you get involved in the firm. It's fascinating to understand the dilemmas that the average individual borrower in Malawi experiences. You're confronted with people who are making decisions about telling an employer that they have AIDS or potentially solving a debt by putting a brother or a child into a form of slavery. These are trade-offs that you and I sitting here in London or, New York—or wherever someone might be—can't imagine.

The Definition of Right and Wrong

We're all too ready to look down on the decisions and question them in terms of right or wrong—not understanding the context, not understanding that in many cases, we're talking about all bad choices. What definition does ethics have when people are deciding between two or three or four horrible choices? You begin to get engaged in an entirely different thought process in terms of investing in giving people the tools to make the best decision, without any judgment as to whether or not they've done the wrong thing. Have you given them the best opportunity to make the best solution that's available to them?

Opportunity International begins to invest in individuals for them to gain self-respect and to have the tools to be independent in their thinking and in their decision making, as well as potentially to create a business or a career, and to begin to bring their family or their village out of poverty. All of this, for me, introduced a whole other realm for thinking about ethics.

Doing Business Ethically

Through that, we get many of our employees to start thinking about these challenges in ways that take us out of the office. In so doing, we open the mind—again, back to our creativity and innovation—to put us in a different time and place, with a whole different set of solutions. When you begin to open your mind that way, you begin to think of new and different ways to approach the problems.

The key lesson ends up being that, as you become an increasingly global company, you cannot take a narrow, self-centered, predetermined definition of right and wrong. A great part of being a learning organization is being a listening and understanding organization. You can't invest in relationships and walk into those relationships with your definition of what is right and wrong. As we travel the globe, as we engage in different corners of this universe in which we live, we have to stop, pause, understand, and then work together and invest in our partner's ability to be a part of the solution.

TAKEAWAYS

⮡ As your company becomes increasingly global, you cannot take a narrow, self-centered, predetermined definition of right and wrong.

⮡ A significant part of being a learning organization is being a listening and understanding organization.

⮡ As you engage in different corners of the world, you have to stop, pause, understand, and then work with and invest in your partner's ability to be part of a solution.

Ethics: The Balance of Information

John Abele

Founder, Boston Scientific Corporation

THIS LESSON IS ABOUT an experience that I had after we were probably at about $100 million in sales. I was invited to participate at an Ethics and Engineering course at the Massachusetts Institute of Technology (MIT). Initially, I was a bit concerned about why they wanted somebody from the industry there and what they wanted to do. It was explained to me that ethics and engineering is a subject that a lot of students are asking about: not just the concept of not wanting to develop guns, but also about a desire to develop things that help the world, not hurt it. Frequently in the development process, there are conflicts that arise, which require ethical decision making.

I was invited as a guinea pig, if you will; the students were asked to write a scenario so the industry person or the senior executive could say how they would deal with it. Usually, since I was in the medical business, they would come up with a problem very much like this one: you have just spent $15 million developing this new product. You've put together a promotional campaign, you've gone through the regulatory process, it's been approved, you have some excited physicians, and you are ready to launch this product two weeks from now. You've already had clinical trials of this product in the field. Now you get a phone call, and you're told that the company has discovered a problem with this product. They are getting poor yields in this one process, and they think that some of the products might fail in the field. What do you do?

I had been concerned because I had thought they were going to present a problem that would be very embarrassing for me to answer. The irony is that the problem was fairly easy to answer. The first thing I told them is that I would understand the problem as much as possible. I would take that product and that problem, and I would go and talk to each one of the users—the people who had been doing these trials for the FDA force and so forth.

I'd say, "Here's the problem, here's what we know, and here's what we don't know. What would you do? Is that something that we should repeal? Is it something that you can manage through, or not?"

What amazed me is that the engineers—the students—were amazed by that. They said, "Oh, we never thought of asking the customers." They thought you would make the decision internally and keep customers uninformed.

When our engineers at Boston Scientific Corporation came to me and said, "We want to understand what your position is if we discover a problem," the first thing I said was, "I want to know about it."

They replied, "If we let you know about it, are you going to recall the product?"

I said, "No, I'm going to find out more information and ask the people who are using the product whether this problem will affect their use, or whether it is something where the benefit of use exceeds the risk of use."

That's the fundamental ethical decision that everybody has to deal with. Think about what a surgeon does. He uses a scalpel to cut people. That cut can be used for good or for bad. Interestingly, the engineers didn't think of that.

Next we talked about the concept of being a whistle-blower. The comment that I made there was that if somebody talks to somebody outside without making a sustained effort to talk inside, shame on him. That person should be thrown in jail, from my point of view. That person has really broken the social contract that you have not only within the organization, but also with all your customers who may depend on this product.

The key is really about balance of information: making sure that all the people in the chain—the manufacturer and the user—understand the risk and the rewards. They must understand all the attributes of how the product can be used or abused to make it work well or not.

TAKEAWAYS

⚘ When confronted with difficult ethical choices, it's a mistake to isolate and manage them away from the people they may affect.

Doing Business Ethically

⚏ To publicize potential product problems before making a sustained effort to address the problems within the community that manufactures and uses the product is to break the social contract of trust both within the manufacturing organization and with customers.

⚏ The key to making ethical decisions regarding product recalls is balancing information: making sure that all the people in the product chain—the manufacturer and the user—understand all the attributes of how the product can be used or abused to make it work well or not.

Business Ethics Is About a Bunch of Small Decisions

Heather Loisel

Vice President, Global Marketing Operations, SAP

I'VE BEEN WORKING for a little more than twenty years now. I still read my university alumni magazine and *Fortune* magazine. I went to a Catholic university

Doing Business Ethically

where I learned to look at both ends of the spectrum in terms of how to make good business decisions. One of the conclusions I've come to is that ethics in business is so important. Whether we're talking about sales and marketing, or whether we're talking about just relationships between people, I think that having ethics in business is about a bunch of small decisions versus a bunch of big ones.

I was working at a company where I was asked to reduce a group from twenty-four people down to twenty-two. The typical way to do this is to look at performance and demand and try to make a rational decision about it. In this situation, there was one person who was on the list and should have been. Then I had another person in the group who was a star performer but happened to be out on short-term disability because he had been diagnosed with cancer. He'd gone through a couple remissions, but it had come back.

I went to my company and said, "I know you want to get me to get from twenty-four to twenty-two, but let me hang out at twenty-three just for a few months. Steve's not coming back. He's still on short-term disability, so he's in my head count, but he's not coming back. He's going to be on long-term disability soon. Why disrupt person number twenty-two's life, too? Let me sit on twenty-three for three or four months. I'll get to your twenty-two. We'll hit the objectives for the company, but I want to be able to do the right thing."

The company came back to me and said, "No, you have to get to twenty-two today."

I said, "Here's the situation." I tried again. "Here's the situation."

They said, "No, you have to get to twenty-two."

When I submitted that spreadsheet, I had listed the person who unfortunately should have been on there, and I put my name on and sent it in. I was fully committed at that point for my name to be on that list.

Now, not everyone can make a decision like that. Who knows if I was really taking a risk or not? But by doing that, they let me stay at twenty-three, and it called attention to Steve's situation. Steve and his wife weren't getting the kind of support that they could have because they didn't know what questions to ask. HR completely rallied around Steve. He did end up dying. He stayed alive long enough to see his daughter born, because that was his goal at that point. The company rallied around, giving him the level of support that he and his wife needed to get through that.

I think there are opportunities throughout a person's career to make small decisions and to negotiate on behalf of customers or employees, or just do in your heart what you feel is the right thing to do. You end up having a positive outcome so that as you look back over a period of time—and I know we all do this—you can say, "I've made a lot of small decisions that were really good ones," as opposed to not holding yourself to the standards that you had when you graduated from college, but the ones you have now after working for twenty years.

TAKEAWAYS

- Practicing ethics in business is about a bunch of small decisions versus a bunch of big ones.

- There are many opportunities throughout a person's career to make small decisions and to negotiate on behalf of customers or employees.

- If you do in your heart what you feel is the right thing to do in each moment, you are more likely to accumulate positive outcomes and maintain the standards with which you began your career.

Do the Right Thing in All Circumstances

Sir David Bell

Director for People, Pearson

THIS IS A SMALL STORY in a way, but when I was being trained as a journalist, one day a little boy fell off the side of a boat in the Thames and drowned. The then-editor of the local paper, the *Oxford Mail*, which I worked for, summoned me and said, "I want you to do this story, but on no account will you intrude on private grief. Therefore I do not wish you to go and get a photograph of this boy, because his parents will be in mourning and I don't want them upset."

I admired that greatly, because that was not the competitive thing to do. The competitive thing to do was to go and knock on the door until you got the picture. What he was doing was saying, "There are standards. The time to test the standards is right at the moment when there's the maximum competitive pressure. I don't really care what the competitive pressure is in this case." The right thing to do was not to disturb that family. That's not how most newspapers would operate today, but I admired that a great deal.

What I took from that is that however strong the competitive pressures, if you believe something is right, you should stick to it. That's really been etched on my memory ever since.

Later on, when I was managing editor of the *Financial Times*, there were always issues that arose in which somebody would say, "Well, do you want me to go and do this?" Always, this would come back into my mind—no. The answer is, whatever the pressure, if it's the wrong thing to do, it's the wrong thing to do.

The lesson is that throughout one's life in business, there are always great pressures to do things for competitive reasons. You're always being tested, morally, as to whether you should do that. The temptation is always to say, "If I don't do it, somebody else will. If I don't get the picture of this young kid, somebody else will." My then-editor's view was: that may happen, and if so, you may lose out. But if it's the wrong thing to do, it's the wrong thing to do. I very strongly believe that.

Ultimately, you benefit from that because people come to trust you and what you do— you didn't do what you believed was wrong. It's a difficult decision, and that was only a tiny example, but these situations crop up all the time.

TAKEAWAYS

⫰ The time to test standards is right at the moment when there's the maximum competitive pressure.

⫰ However strong the competitive pressures, if you believe something is right, you should stick to it.

⫰ Ultimately, you benefit from sticking to your principles, because people come to trust you and what you do.

—◆◆◆—

Setting the Right Tone at the Top

—◆◆◆—

Sir Michael Rake

Chairman, BT Group

IN THE LAST FEW YEARS, when we look at what's happened in the business world, there's been a complete breakdown of trust. There's been a complete breakdown of trust in the operation of the capital markets and a complete breakdown of trust in chief executives and the way they operate. The assumption has been that everyone operates out of a sense of greed, if not dishonesty, to enrich themselves at the expense of others. This is what's happened as a result of all the corporate scandals that we've seen, not only in the United States, but also in the United Kingdom. Of course, as a result of that, we've seen an enormous amount of regulation, legislation, litigation, and rule making.

The reason we've had these problems—this lack of trust and these cases of extreme behavior and extreme greed—is actually because of the culture of the organization, in my view. I've seen it in many companies we've investigated. Yes, things can go wrong from a control and environmental point of view, but if you come down to the culture, often you see that it's the tone at the top—the tone that an individual leader sets—that is incredibly important to the way the whole organization works.

One of the things that we all need to understand when we take responsibility for public companies—whether we're advisers to them, auditors to them, or nonexecutive directors in them—is how important this issue is. Because if you don't have the right tone or the right culture, it's amazing how even intelligent people will somehow become overwhelmed by that culture. Clearly that's the case with Enron and in many other companies that you've seen, where the culture went wrong at the top.

I think this leads into real leadership by example, because one of the key things leaders have to understand is that they're very visible. Anything they do is really exaggerated in the communication of any company, so their attitude toward "living what they say" is very important, as is their attitude toward the basic values.

How do people behave with each other? What is the sense of integrity? What is the sense of respect for people within the organization, whatever their level? Do they have real respect for them, not just have a charter? Enron had an enormously laudable charter of values in corporate social responsibility, but actually underneath that it was almost a smoke screen for abuse.

Doing Business Ethically

What you need to have is people seeing that it isn't a charter of values or corporate social responsibility: it's actually meant to be the way that people at the top really behave—to live the values of the organization.

Not only is corporate social responsibility the right thing to do in the communities in which we operate; the business case is enormously important as well. It adds value to your brand, it adds prestige and pride to your people, it aids recruitment and retention, and it also creates the right culture within a capitalist world. The only reason we have capitalism and public companies is so they create wealth for many, not just a few. Trust in organizations has to be seen and believed by employees, regulators, politicians, and journalists. The company has to act it out; it has to really deliver and live it— and that always starts, in my experience, with the example of the guy or the lady at the top.

In investigations we've done into companies and individuals where things have gone wrong, what's stunning is that very often you find that within an organization where the culture's wrong or the tone at the top is wrong, that the individual has crossed from white, to gray, to black. Most of them have to operate in the gray a lot of the time, and often when they cross into the black and they've actually committed an illegal act, they haven't realized it. When you talk to them and interview them, you find that because the culture of the organization's gone wrong, the tone at the top is wrong. Because of the aggressiveness with which the targets are set or the way in which their achievement of those targets is rewarded, intelligent, honest people suddenly think that this is OK; within that environment, it seems to be OK. It isn't OK; they've actually done something that is illegal, amoral, or criminal.

You have to create an approach that actually rewards the right culture. You have to have some role models: people who are promoted and seen to be those who demonstrate these values, that integrity, and that approach to others. You have to be seen to

Doing Business Ethically

frankly deal with people who, having been properly counseled or advised, still do not adopt those values. However clever they might be, however technically brilliant they might be, if they're creating an environment where the culture is wrong, then they're going to be a net deficit to the organization. You need to seriously think about removing them. It's like a cancer: it creates an environment where people think that's the way you have to be in order to survive or to succeed, and that's very damaging for an organization. I'm not saying, obviously, that every case ends like Enron, but you see a lot of companies that fail and become inefficient when people become unmotivated.

In a large organization, you have to work very hard at ensuring that people understand these values and the way they should operate. The basic lesson here is the huge responsibility of any leader to set the right tone at the top, to live the values the company espouses, and to really lead by example.

TAKEAWAYS

- If an organization and its leaders do not set the right tone or create the right culture, it's amazing how even intelligent people will somehow become overwhelmed by that culture.

- Within an organization where the culture's wrong, or the tone at the top is wrong, you often find that when an individual actually commits an illegal act, he doesn't realize it.

- In order to successfully create the right culture, you must establish role models: people who are promoted and seen to be those who demonstrate ethical values and integrity.

Integrity and Trust Deliver Results

Gerry Roche

Senior Chairman, Heidrick & Struggles

INTEGRITY USED to be something that was taken for granted; it was assumed. But these days, the number one requirement that boards are looking for from people is integrity. It almost seems a shame to have to say it, but trustworthiness and integrity are at the top of the list. There's a story that tells a little about integrity and drives the point home.

We were competing to get the Disney search for a new CEO. I was facing the board of directors of Disney, and I was asked if we could get Jim McNerney, a guy I'd put into 3M. He used to run jet engines at GE, and we put him in as the chairman and CEO of 3M. He's a terrific guy and one of the best general managers in the world and is recognized as such. The Disney board, being fully aware of how good McNerney is, asked me whether he was somebody that I could approach if I were given the search.

I replied, "No, I can't approach him. I put him in, so it's a violation of our ethics for us to take anybody out that we put in."

They said, "If we visit him ourselves or put in a call to him, and got a flicker of interest from him, could we then turn it over to you?"

I said, "Absolutely not. I can't lift a finger to help Jim McNerney get out of 3M, and that's final. As a matter of fact, if you do get a flicker of hope out of him, I don't even want to know about it."

So, that was my answer, and I thought, "Well, that took care of Disney for Heidrick & Struggles."

As it turned out, we were awarded the assignment. I had the gall to ask Disney, "Why did you pick us?" One of the reasons was that one of our competitors had been asked the same question about somebody that they had put into a situation.

They had said, "No, we couldn't take him out . . ." But then they volunteered, ". . . but if you call him yourself and get a nibble out of him, then we can work around it."

Boom! They didn't know it, but they killed themselves with that comment, because the very thing that Disney wanted more than anything else was integrity. They sell, show, and preach integrity. They felt that my answer may have cost us the search, but I was willing to risk that for the honesty and integrity of the situation.

When you think about our business and what we do, the number one thing we have to develop with anybody—clients, candidates, sources, references—is trust. We get Disney's board to totally open up and tell us all their corporate secrets. They tell us more than they tell anyone else—including their employees—because they have to give us the picture. They give us all their corporate secrets, an enormous fee, and an expense account with no limits. We can travel all over the world, spending whatever we want to, staying wherever we want to, developing candidates on this. So, what does the Disney board need most from us to be worthy of that? Trust. There's no way you can overemphasize the need for trust.

TAKEAWAYS

⊰ The number one requirement boards are looking for from people today is integrity.

Integrity and Trust

⚜ You must maintain your honesty and integrity even at the risk of losing new business.

⚜ The need for trust in business transactions and relationships cannot be overemphasized.

Never Lose Integrity

Blythe McGarvie

CEO and Founder, Leadership for
International Finance

THE MOST IMPORTANT lesson I've learned is: you have to keep your integrity. That's the one thing you can't lose. Your reputation will precede you no matter what you do, and keeping your integrity is the most important thing. People often say, "What do you mean by *integrity*? That's such an overused word. Sure, that sounds like *mom* or *apple pie*. Of course you need to keep your integrity." Well, I call it "your values in your innermost core," and I'll give you an example.

When I first became the chief financial officer at BIC Group, the pen company based in France, I had only been there a week. My dishes hadn't even crossed the Atlantic Ocean to come and join me in Paris. I was there at work, and the boss—the chairman and president of the company— said to me, "It's July. I want you to release earnings in two weeks, before everyone disappears for the holidays." They had never released earnings in July. They always had done that in September. I said, "Let me go back and check and see where we are on the closing of the books, and I'll get back to you in about an hour."

To my amazement, I found out we didn't even have a balance sheet that had balanced for the last four months. We didn't have the proper records. I said, "How can I release earnings without a good balance sheet, because that obviously affects the P&L?" I went to talk to the chairman, and I said,

Never Lose Integrity

"I can't do this." I'm sitting there thinking that I have three options. One, I can be a whistle-blower and tell the community this major company does not have financial controls or financial statements; you've got to understand this. Or two, I could quit. I could say, "Wait a minute, this is a company that does not have the types of controls or the reputation and integrity that I expect a company this size to have, because it will reflect on my own integrity." Or three, I could try and find a way to solve the problem.

So, I talked to the chairman. I went to our public accounting firm and talked to the major partner there. I said, "We have a major issue here. We need to get some books cleaned up. We need to get some things closed. We only have four weeks to do it." We agreed not to release earnings in July, so the pressure was off me until September, but we really hurried and worked a lot of long hours to be ready for a September release.

The lesson I learned here is that instead of just doing what your new boss wants you

to do, think about it first, because it's going
to reflect on you. I've changed jobs in my
career. I've gone to different companies.
Within a company, I've changed jobs. It's
only natural to want to please your boss.
The first thing you want to do is make your
boss look good and make sure that he's
happy with your results. But never do it at
the expense of what you believe is right.

Other people were closing the books.
The prior CFO, who had been fired, was
closing the books. I don't know how he
could have done it for the other few
months, because he was giving out P&L
information that was not correct. But I
couldn't do it. Personally, I wanted to make
sure that I could hold my head up high and
explain to the investors and the shareholders, and the family—because the family was a
major shareholder in BIC—that we had
numbers that you could trust, that were
credible, and that had been checked and
balanced. I think it's so important.

This was my dream job—living and
working in France with a major consumer

company—and I actually thought about getting back on the plane and leaving. It would
have been a mistake. To find something
wrong and then leave is not the answer because you're just letting it fester until somebody else might have the courage to speak up
and to stand out.

Integrity is the only thing we have. We're
born with it; we learn it. We learn it very
early in life. Sometimes we might fail. We
experience things that might rekindle that
integrity, but you always have to be vigilant,
because it's the only thing you have. And if
you lose it, it takes a long time—if at all—for
you to gain it back.

TAKEAWAYS

🔖 It's only natural to want to please your
boss, but never do it at the expense of
what you believe is right.

Doing Business Ethically

⚐ To find something wrong in a new
  company and then leave is not the answer, because you're just letting the
  problem fester until somebody else
  has the courage to speak up and to
  stand out.

⚐ Always be vigilant regarding your integrity, because if you lose it, it takes a
  long time for you to gain it back, if you
  ever do.

Credibility Is Fragile and Needs to Be Protected

Ying Yeh

*Chairman and President, North Asia Region,
Eastman Kodak Company*

THERE'S A SAYING THAT reputation
is anyone's second life. And credibility is
actually any enterprise's second life. It is
very important to understand that if, in

any company or enterprise, you don't have credibility, your customers and the market will not trust and believe you. When we first came into China, we knew this was one thing we would follow, not only by Chinese law, but importantly, because we needed to let the society and the market understand the Kodak way and the Kodak standard.

In the early days, for sensitized goods, the tariff was very high. We did not manufacture in China, so a lot of semifinished product needed to be imported. There was one shipment—actually inside the shipment— where the declaration form specified six master rolls. They are huge. And we enjoyed basically the green-light treatment, so the shipment went straight into our factory, such that we didn't need to clear customs. When a very low-ranking logistics clerk brought it back into our warehouse and opened it up, the shipment contained not six, but ten rolls. As it turned out, those four extra master rolls translated to close to $1 million in U.S. tariff.

Credibility Needs to Be Protected

That was a Friday afternoon. The clerk didn't say anything. He immediately sealed the container, sent it straight back to customs, and told customs that we made a mistake. Customs was already closed at that time. Most of the registration office clerks had gone. We were told to come back Monday.

So, on Monday, the clerk told his supervisor, and then we went to the accounts department with a check in hand. Before noon, it was paid back to customs. There were people in U.S. Customs who had been in that business for forty-some years. A lot of them were shocked; they had never heard of such a thing. And as it turned out, a lot of people asked us about this story. They asked, number one, "Did the clerk get punished because he didn't even report to the manager level before he made the decision?"

We said, "No, of course not. That was his job, that's what the training is all about, and he did the right thing."

The follow-up question was, "Was he rewarded?"

Doing Business Ethically

And we said, "Of course not, because he just basically did what he was trained to do."

It is stories like this—we didn't have a camera there to record it, or any reporters to report the story—that, by word of mouth, went straight through the entire customs system and actually later on was specially featured in an internal publication of the Chinese Customs Service.

So, for this, people trust us. But credibility is a very fragile thing. It can take you years to build, but it can be destroyed overnight. Once you build your credibility, it's very important that you guard it religiously.

TAKEAWAYS

---

‡ If your company or enterprise does not have credibility, your customers and the market will not trust and believe you.

Credibility Needs to Be Protected

⚄ Providing your people with proper training means they will know exactly what to do when faced with an ethical dilemma.

⚄ Credibility is fragile; it can take years to build but be destroyed overnight.

Pick the Right Moment to Fight Prejudice

Marilyn Carlson Nelson

Chairman, Carlson Companies

MY EXPERIENCE as a woman has maybe required of me perseverance, resilience, a fair amount of drive, and a bit of creativity, and then from time to time, has forced me to be sure that I kept my priorities in order. An early example was coming out of Smith

Doing Business Ethically

College with a degree with honors in international economics, and having studied in Europe at the Sorbonne and in Geneva at the Graduate School of Political Science, and finding that, in those days, I could've been a teacher or a nurse. I wanted to be a security analyst or a registered representative, and there weren't even women investment bankers yet in Minnesota.

I finally convinced them that I could be a security analyst, that I had the training to be a security analyst. Then they came, and they talked me through all the protocol and what I needed to do, etc. We had a very hot market here in the upper Midwest, so I was going to be the local analyst for this local hot market. I wrote my first paper, and everybody was excited about it, my first recommendation. And then I saw what they published. It didn't say "Marilyn Nelson"; it said "M. C. Nelson."

I said, "What's the M. C.?"

They said, "Oh, we forgot to tell you. We can't let them know you're a woman. No one would buy stock recommended by a *woman*."

Fight Prejudice

So, I had a couple of choices. My daughters say, "Why didn't you get up and walk out?" Well, if I'd gotten up and walked out, I would've given up a very good job. I loved doing what I was doing. I decided that they could call me anything. I guess that's what George Elliott said when she named herself George—as did some of the painters who have given themselves male names through history.

My early experience was that I should try to do the job to the best of my ability, that I should spend less time being angry and indignant, and to channel any anger or indignation I felt into staying awake a little longer, going the extra mile, trying to do the job better. There was a lot of discussion about whether women had to do it better. Well, we sure had to do it *as* well. And in some cases, you felt unsafe unless you really tried to do it better.

I learned a big lesson then, which was, did I want to *do* something or *be* something? And that put me in very good stead along the way, because at various points in my career, I was *doing* it, and maybe a male was taking credit for it or *being* it. Along the way, I developed a lot of skills, and I learned that performing is important, that performing has its own rewards. Then over time, it gave me much more confidence to take a stand when the moment was right, and I decided a compromise was too great, and I really had to negotiate a different kind of relationship. But I was negotiating from real strength, not from emotion, not from anger.

I think for anyone—whether you're a woman or a man—if you find at any point in your career that the system you're in is in some way forcing you to compromise, I think you need first to be brutally honest with yourself. Are they right? The fact is that you can rationalize, "I'm as good as someone else. I'm this and that." But maybe check it out. Do your own personal 360. Ask some people, "You know, I'm being criticized for this," or "I wasn't given this promotion, and I think it was prejudice of one sort or another, but what is your impression?" Check it out.

Fight Prejudice

Now, if you're legitimately in an environment where things are not fair and you feel you have an opportunity to change that environment, stay. I do believe it's totally appropriate. Do not let yourself ever have a victim mentality. If you catch yourself feeling victimized, take personal accountability and take action today. Either get out or change it or confront somebody, but if you start to become a victim, it's a sickness as deadly as a cancer.

TAKEAWAYS

🔖 Whether you're a woman or a man, if you feel compromised at any point in your career, you need to be as honest with yourself as possible and objective enough to consider the viewpoints of others.

Doing Business Ethically

⚔ If you find yourself in an environment
where conditions are not fair and
you have an opportunity to change
them, it's totally appropriate to stay
and do so.

⚔ Do not ever let yourself have a victim
mentality; take personal accountability
and action, whether by leaving a bad
situation or by confronting it.

It's Always Your Place to Say Something

Mark Goyder

Founder Director, Tomorrow's Company

THE YEAR IS 1979. I'm in my mid-twenties, had just gotten married, and I'm in the paper mill in Kent where I had recently been appointed personnel manager. During the summer shutdown, a great deal of work is going on, but the health and safety officer is on holiday. So, I have the added responsibility of being the acting health and safety officer. Into my office walks the six-foot-tall plant engineer, who has been at the company since he was an apprentice. He's in his early sixties, a figure of great authority in the mill. Nobody says no to Fred.

Fred comes in and says, "Oh, you ought to know, there's been a bit of an accident at the power station. But it's alright. Nobody's been hurt. It's just an incident, really, that happens from time to time. There's no need to report it. We don't need to do that. We've never done it that way here. Just so that you know about it, but you need take no further action."

I'm left wondering whether there isn't something slightly odd about this and what my responsibilities are as acting health and safety officer. Luckily enough, I had my father, with whom I often talked about my work. I phoned him up and said, "What do you make of this?"

He said, "I don't like the sound of it. What's the legal position?"

Your Place to Say Something

I said, "Looking at the books, it looks to me as though this kind of thing should be reported."

He said, "It's very simple. You have all the authority you need. If you think that's the legal position, just put it in writing. You'll find the rest falls into place."

So, I took his advice and put into writing that I judged this to be a reportable incident. The next time Fred saw me, he looked at me with daggers in his eyes. He was very angry at the meeting where we discussed the incident. But there was nothing he could do. Incidentally, he treated me with a lot more respect thereafter.

The lesson I learned was that businesses desperately need to put in place the kind of framework of values that a young and inexperienced person like me can actually refer to and say, "I'm sure this isn't the way we do things around here." In the absence of that, the chances are that decisions will be made on the basis of who has the strongest personality, not on the basis of what is either the right thing to do or, indeed, the best thing to do from the point of view of risk and reputation.

The first thing is that it is almost always a good idea to pause before committing yourself. The second thing I've learned from making wrong and right decisions at different times in my career is that the times I've gotten it wrong is when I believed somebody who told me, "Don't worry; that's the way we always do it." That's one of the most dangerous things to say, because what you are doing is consenting in some way to an implied agenda that you don't really understand and of which you don't really know the consequences.

You have to take responsibility for the agenda, and if you don't understand, that is not your fault; that's other people's fault. Until you understand and are clear, keep asking questions and keep challenging others. In all the corporate tragedies one reads about, there is a common thread, which is: somebody out there knew there was something odd, but they didn't think it was their place to say anything.

It's *always* your place to say something.

TAKEAWAYS

⚎ Businesses need to put into place a framework of values that employees can refer to in order to ensure that decisions are made on the basis of what is the right thing to do or the best thing to do, rather than on the basis of who has the strongest personality.

⚎ When confronted with an ethical dilemma, it is a good idea to pause for consideration before committing yourself to a course of action.

⚎ It is always your place to say something, to ask questions, if something seems wrong.

—■◆◆■—

Don't Listen to Rumor

—■◆◆■—

David Gonski

Chairman, Coca-Cola Amatil

IN MY CAREER, which is now well over thirty years in business, I've had many challenges. Often you remember the challenges earlier in your career because, frankly, the risk was even higher then. You had no reputation to lose, but on the other hand, you might never have a reputation of any strength if you didn't fix it.

Doing Business Ethically

It was around 1980 or 1981 that, as a
partner in a large law firm, which is where
I was in those days, I devised one of the first
takeover bids under the new legislation.
It was a bold idea, which I cleared with the
senior partner. The two of us were very sure
that this was the way to go. What happened
was that the press disagreed vehemently. On
the front page of the business paper every
day, they lampooned us, the legislation, and
our client, that we should be allowed to be
so clever and do things that, perhaps in
their view, they felt shouldn't be done.

One of our most senior partners summoned a meeting of not only me but also
my senior partner and the senior partner of
the entire firm. I remember that meeting as
if it were yesterday. We sat in his big office
on the corner, which is the one I aspired to
and never got. As he looked out over the
harbor, he said, "I've been talking to a few
people in the regulators' office, and they
think that our firm has done something
enormously wrong here. They feel that
you are flouting the law, and they feel that

our firm shouldn't be involved in this sort of thing."

The way he put it suggested not only that my most senior partner and I had let down the firm, but also that this was a watershed. If we didn't go ahead with this, he'd be happy and we'd look like idiots in my view, but we would get on with life. If we kept going, maybe we should keep going in another firm. I remember our most senior partner sat there and listened to this whole thing and said not a word. He was the man who'd built the firm. He looked at us, and I thought, "Here it comes. I have been a partner two years, which was a very nice time, and now I'm going out to do gardening or something."

He looked at me and my senior partner and said, "In my experience, if people are using rumors that they don't like you, it means you're getting at them. Keep going. You're obviously on the right side." He walked out of the room, which of course left the other senior partner in terrible trouble, so he decided to walk out of the room,

which I found quite interesting because
it was his office.

We sat there, the two of us, and realized
a lesson. You don't listen to rumor. If
somebody, be it a regulator or a judge or
whomever, is concerned about what you're
doing, they tell you. Then you judge and
you do what has to be done. The second lesson is, you obviously think through what is
right. If you believe you've done right, you
don't listen to rumor to stop what you've
done. This was a lesson that I took forward
from there, but I have to admit there was a
third lesson. I'd let what I felt was my legal
intelligence take over what I was doing. I'd
given what I regarded was a black letter law
solution, which titivated my thinking. But
actually, I should have sat back and asked
myself, "Should this be done?" We were very
lucky. A month later, our client decided,
for other commercial reasons, not to pro-
ceed, and the matter all fell away.

I'm not proud of that event, but I learned
twenty-eight years ago three enormous

lessons. To summarize those lessons: make sure that you think about what you're doing; don't be too clever; think about the consequences. Second, don't listen to rumor. Rumor is faceless men and women who are saying nothing. Third, remember that if someone has something to say, they'll tell you and you deal with it. Also most particularly, you must feel right about what you're doing, because if you *don't* feel right, it often *isn't* right.

TAKEAWAYS

- Make sure you think about your actions; don't be too clever; think about the consequences.

- Don't listen to rumor. If somebody is concerned about what you're doing,

Doing Business Ethically

they will tell you; then you can make a
decision and do what has to be done.

✠ You must feel right about what you're
doing, because if you *don't* feel right, it
often *isn't* right.

Profits and Principles

Dame Anita Roddick

Founder, The Body Shop International

THE CYNICISM IN THIS country is
unparalleled, and it takes on a strange robe
or cover. The cover is insight; to be cynical
means you have insight. And it's lies; it's
just lack of moral courage. I saw more cynicism in the financial press—the cynicism
that says you have no value unless you just

talk finances, that economic values are the only values in this world.

I remember a case in point when we opened a soap factory in Glasgow in a place called Easterhouse, which was arguably then the worst housing area in Western Europe. We wanted to build our soap factory there; we wanted to make it a shining example of really progressive factories: the best pay in the area, the best working conditions, the best health and security and education; everything. We also wanted to put 25 percent of the profits back into the community.

Well, we did. And I thought, "We're on the side of the angels now." Not for the financial media, which really, really took exception to this and said we were stealing money from our shareholders' investment. There's nothing in law that says you have to maximize your profit; there's nothing at all that says that. And I thought, this isn't about making a company brilliant or brave or exciting; this is about just being obsessed with one group of people who

are investing in you financially—could
be £10, could be £100—but they would
have more strength than the people
who've worked fifteen, twenty years
with you.

My retort to the media was, "Up your
bum. This is the way we're doing this; this is
the way our company's being run." Whether
setting up an adventure playground or a
drop-in center for the elderly, we chose to
put our money back into the community.
But it was a fight; it was a fight all the time
with the media. I think it is the terrorism
of the "or." You can either be one thing *or*
you've got to be another. I think it's the
genius of the "and." I think you can do
both. The Quakers did it: brilliantly successful, financially resolute, and never
lied—can you imagine that in business
now?—never cheated, never stole, gave
money to the community, built towns and
communities, and cared for the people that
they employed.

We were learning from them. It's a
very interesting methodology, and

Doing Business Ethically

John F. Kennedy said it brilliantly. He said, "The great enemy of the truth is very often not the lie: deliberate, contrived, and dishonest, but the myth: persistent, persuasive, and unrealistic." This notion that you can't be socially responsible and profitable isn't true. I think that's the myth. You can. You're more frugal, you don't waste, you're more environmentally aware, you're more transparent, you're more diligent, and you don't waste money.

TAKEAWAYS

- The belief that the only value is economic value is a form of cynicism.

- "The great enemy of truth is very often not the lie: deliberate, contrived and dishonest, but the

Profits and Principles

myth: persistent, persuasive and unrealistic."—*John F. Kennedy*

🙰 The notion that you can't be socially responsible and profitable is a myth.

Beyond Business
as Usual

Lynda Gratton

Professor of Management Practice
London Business School

ONE OF THE INTERESTING things that
I do, as an academic, is interview all sorts of
interesting people, very often chief executives, about their companies. So, when I
write a case and then a book about a company, I start off by spending a considerable

amount of time with their senior team, asking them their thoughts and beliefs about an organization and what it means to be leading it.

One of the interviews that I've reflected on for some time is with a man called John Browne, who was the chief executive of BP. One of the things that he said to me and the colleague who was interviewing him was, "Organizations have to believe in something that's greater than the return on capital employed."

Now, I thought that was a very interesting thing to say, because actually, the analysts who are looking at a company are really interested in the return on capital employed. They're really interested in whether they make a £9 billion profit a year or not. But the point that he made is, "Organizations have to be a force for good." And those words—"a force for good"—have really stuck in my mind.

When we went and spoke to the employees of BP, really went down and talked to young people and people doing middle management jobs, and said, "Tell us about BP," the words "force for good" came out quite a lot. I think the interesting thing about the force for good is it wasn't just a piece of rhetoric. It's so easy for a CEO to say that an organization has to play an important role in society. Here it was actually reality.

So, all the way through BP we saw examples of things that BP was doing to try and address some of the challenges it faced. In talking with John Browne, what I began to realize was that the leaders of large organizations have enormous responsibility. I remember Rodney Chase, one of the deputies of John Browne, saying to me, "BP has revenues that are larger than a small country in the world." These are massive institutions; they have massive power. What was very striking here was that a senior team was taking responsibility for some of the power they had and was actually thinking about what they could do.

So, the lesson that I learned is that it is possible, even in a world that looks at return

on capital employed, to talk about things
that are greater than that. It is possible to
talk about a force for good. It is possible to
engage employees in a conversation about
what an organization can be, that is greater
than simply its monetary resources. Getting
that balance between business as usual and
trying to do something inspirational is incredibly difficult. I recall the anger in John
Browne's eyes when he said that when BP
initially talked about a force for good—in
fact they rebranded BP to mean Beyond
Petroleum—he said the analysts were pretty
cynical about it. They thought it was just
another PR gimmick. The only way he man-
aged to keep that balance was because of the
courage that he has and that those around
him have.

Actually, only the most courageous chief
executives are able to also talk about the
inspiration for the future. It's not an easy
thing to do. It's not an easy thing to talk to
analysts about. It's not an easy thing to talk
to your employees about. But I believe it's

absolutely crucial. Talking to chief executives around the world, I realize it's very easy for them to be completely transfixed by the role they have as administrators, often running enormous companies with people right across the world.

But I think what separates the great CEOs is their capacity to inspire others. What I thought was very interesting about John Browne's work at BP is that he was seen by those around him as an inspirational leader, somebody who was able to talk about things that were beyond business as usual.

TAKEAWAYS

- Organizations have to believe in something that's greater than the return on capital employed; they have to be a force for good.

Doing Business Ethically

⚔ Only the most courageous chief executives are equal to the difficult task of talking to analysts and employees about the inspiration for the future.

⚔ What distinguishes great CEOs is their capacity to inspire others, to talk about things beyond business as usual.

Stick to Your Principles

Clive Mather

Former President and CEO, Shell Canada

I SPENT FIVE YEARS in South Africa between 1986 and 1991. Going back to 1986, I recall an extraordinary time of challenge. My company, Shell, was targeted by the anti-apartheid movement that was very, very keen, of course, that major corporations, such as ourselves, should leave South

Doing Business Ethically

Africa in order to undermine the apartheid government. Our view was different. Our view was that we offered greater advantage to the people of South Africa by staying than by going, and that through our presence, our corporate behavior, and our innovation, we could do more for the country. But the politics were raw.

In South Africa, there was growing violence, and outside South Africa, companies like ours were targeted. I well recall Barclays leaving, and Mobil, a sister oil company—an American company—was also forced to leave. So, when my family and I arrived in Cape Town in 1986, we left behind all manner of difficulty in Europe with service stations being bombed, and so on. As we drove from the airport into the city center, I well remember fires around and people in semi-riot—hugely difficult conditions.

Of course, over time that changed. When we left, we were able to celebrate the election of Nelson Mandela as president, and we were able to see the first fruits of democracy really start to emerge. But it wasn't easy.

Stick to Your Principles

I have nothing but admiration for all of those who took part in the struggle to end apartheid. I saw firsthand the real pain that they had to bear: mistreatment, abuse, harassment, and so on. Even my colleagues at work were in the same position. It was ironic in a way that we would be having as much trouble with the government locally as we were actually having from our opponents overseas.

So, why did we hang on? People say, "Wouldn't it have been easier to go?" And, of course, it would have been. But we did hang on. We believed that by staying we offered more; we believed we could demonstrate through our employment practices, our business ethics, and our promotion of a just society that ultimately we added more to South Africa by remaining. We also believed that conceding to violence is a dangerous precedent. If you pull away from South Africa simply because somebody doesn't like you being there, what would happen in other countries where people may have similar views? There will always be those who are in opposition to governments or countries from time to time.

So, we stuck it out, and we're really glad we did. I suppose the most moving part of it of all was after I had left, and President Mandela was celebrating one particular new development that Shell had put in place in the Eastern Cape. This involved bringing solar panels to generate electricity to rural communities that couldn't otherwise afford electricity. As he opened that particular facility, he was very generous in his tribute to Shell for having stuck it out through all those years, to be there as the new society blossomed.

Stick to your principles is a simple phrase but so, so important. In South Africa, we applied our corporate values to a very difficult situation, and we stuck with it against terrific odds at times. We held on to what we believed and, in the event, it came right. And I believe it always will. It's never easy to predict the time frame, but if you believe in what you're doing, hang onto it. In the end, you'll be glad you did.

TAKEAWAYS

- 🖎 It is possible for a company to have significant cultural impact where it does business through its employment practices, its business ethics, and the promotion of a just society.

- 🖎 Conceding to violence is a dangerous precedent. If you pull away from a country simply because somebody doesn't like you being there, what would happen in other countries where people may have similar views?

- 🖎 It's never easy to predict the time frame, but if you believe in what you're doing, hang onto it. In the end, you'll be glad you did.

⊰ ABOUT THE ⊱
CONTRIBUTORS

John Abele is the Cofounder of Boston Scientific Corporation, the worldwide developer, manufacturer, and marketer of medical devices. Mr. Abele has been driving the advancement of less-invasive medical technology for more than twenty-five years.

The history of Boston Scientific began in the late 1960s, when Mr. Abele acquired an equity interest in Medi-tech, Inc., a research and development company focused on developing alternatives to traditional surgery, where he served as president. In 1979, Mr. Abele partnered with Pete Nicholas to buy Medi-tech, and together they formed Boston Scientific Corporation. Since its public offering in 1992, Boston Scientific has undergone an aggressive acquisition strategy, assembling the lines of business that allow it to continue to be a leader in the medical industry. Mr. Abele has been a Director of Boston Scientific since 1979.

Mr. Abele serves as Director of Color Kinetics, Inc., a leader in designing and marketing innovative lighting systems based on light-emitting diode (LED) technology. He has held the Chairmanship of FIRST (For Inspiration and Recognition of Science and Technology) Foundation since 2002.

About the Contributors

Sir David Bell is a Director of Pearson, an international media company. He is also Chairman of the Financial Times Group, having been Chief Executive of the *Financial Times* since 1993.

In July 1998, Sir David was appointed Pearson's Director for People with responsibility for the recruitment, motivation, development, and reward of employees across the Pearson Group. In addition, he is a Director of *The Economist*, the Vitec Group plc, and The Windmill Partnership.

Sir David is a Chairman of Common Purpose International, Crisis, Sadler's Wells, and the International Youth Foundation. He was also Chairman of the Millennium Bridge Trust (1995–2000), which was responsible for conceiving the first new bridge across the Thames in one hundred years.

Sir David was educated at Cambridge University and the University of Pennsylvania.

Marilyn Carlson Nelson is the Chairman of Carlson Companies.

Ms. Carlson Nelson began working with Carlson Companies in 1968. In March 1998, she was named President and CEO. In addition, she took on the Chairmanship in 1999. Though she stepped down as CEO in 2008, Ms. Carlson Nelson remains as Chairman of Carlson Companies. In this role, she leads one of the largest, privately held companies in the United States, which is the parent corporation of a global group of integrated companies specializing in business and leisure travel, and hotel, restaurant, cruise, and marketing services.

About the Contributors

In 2002, Ms. Carlson Nelson was appointed by President Bush to chair the National Women's Business Council, a position she held until 2005. She is a member of the International Business Council of the World Economic Forum, and in 2004 cochaired the forum's annual meeting in Davos, Switzerland. Also in 2004, she was selected by *Forbes* magazine as one of "The World's 100 Most Powerful Women."

Ms. Carlson Nelson is on the boards of Exxon Mobil Corporation and the Mayo Clinic Foundation. In addition, she is on the Board of Overseers of the Curtis L. Carlson School of Management at the University of Minnesota.

David Gonski is the Chairman of Coca-Cola Amatil Ltd., the largest nonalcoholic beverage company in the Pacific Rim. In addition to bottling and distributing the iconic Coca-Cola brand, the company is actively pursuing the high-growth health and wellness sector.

Mr. Gonski was born in South Africa; he and his family moved to Australia when he was seven years old. He graduated with degrees of bachelor of commerce and bachelor of law from the University of New South Wales. By age twenty-five, he had become a partner at the firm of Freehills, where he worked from 1977 to 1986. Thereafter he became a corporate adviser in the firm of Wentworth Associates, now part of the Investec group.

Joining the board of Coca-Cola Amatil in October 1997, Mr. Gonski is Chairman of the

About the Contributors

Related Party Committee and the Nominations Committee. He is a member of the Audit & Risk, Compensation, and Compliance and Social Responsibility Committees.

Mr. Gonski is one of Australia's most prominent business leaders and philanthropists. In addition to being Chairman of Coca-Cola Amatil, he is Chairman of Investec Bank (Australia) Ltd., and ASX Ltd., and is a Director of the Westfield Group and Singapore Airlines. He is also Chairman of Sydney Grammar School and the National E-Health Transition Authority.

In 2002, Mr. Gonski was appointed an Officer of the Order of Australia for service to the community through Australian visual and performing arts organizations, through the development of government policy, and through the promotion of corporate sponsorship for the arts and for charitable organizations. His former roles have included Chairman of the Australia Council for the Arts, Councilor for the Australia Business Arts Foundation, and President of the Art Gallery of New South Wales. In 2007, Mr. Gonski was made a Companion of the Order of Australia. He received the Centenary Medal in 2003.

In 2005, Mr. Gonski was elected Chancellor of the University of New South Wales, the first alumnus to hold that position, for a four-year term. The University Council voted unanimously to reappoint Mr. Gonski to a second term, which runs until 2013.

About the Contributors

Mark Goyder is the Founder Director of Tomorrow's Company, a research and education charity based in the United Kingdom.

After fifteen years as a manager in manufacturing businesses, Mr. Goyder initiated the Royal Society of Arts and Commerce (RSA) Tomorrow's Company Inquiry and subsequently founded the business-led Tomorrow's Company. Over the past ten years, he has inspired and challenged the boards, leaders, and managers of leading large and small companies with his clear vision and his practical insights into the changing agenda for leadership, governance, and stakeholder relationships.

In addition, Mr. Goyder holds a number of other positions in various organizations, including British Airways Corporate Responsibility Board, BT Leadership Advisory Panel, Camelot Advisory Panel for Social Responsibility, and Judge for the Unipart group Mark in Action Awards. In June 2004, he was named Director of the Month by *Director* magazine, and he won the IMS Millenium award for best speaker.

Lynda Gratton is the Professor of Management Practice at the London Business School. In this role, she directs the school's executive program: Human Resource Strategy in Transforming Organizations. She is considered one of the world's authorities on people in organizations and actively advises companies around the world.

About the Contributors

A trained psychologist, Professor Gratton worked for British Airways for several years as an occupational psychologist and then became Director of HR Strategy at PA Consulting Group. From 1992 to 2002, she led the Leading Edge Research Consortium.

Professor Gratton's book, *Living Strategy*, originally published in 2000, has been translated into more than fifteen languages and rated by U.S. CEOs as one of the most important books of the year. Her more recent book, *The Democratic Enterprise*, was described by the *Financial Times* as a work of important scholarship. Her latest book, published in 2007, is *Hot Spots: Why Some Teams, Workplaces, and Organizations Buzz with Energy—and Others Don't*.

In 2005, Professor Gratton was appointed the Director of the Lehman Centre for Women in Business. In 2007, she was included in *The Times'* list of the top fifty business thinkers in the world.

Heather Loisel is Vice President of Global Marketing Operations, SAP AG, a leading provider of business software.

Before assuming this role, Ms. Loisel was the Vice President of Field Marketing for SAP Americas, leading the delivery of marketing content and demand generation to customers and prospects in North and Latin America. Before that, she served as the Vice President of Proposal and Knowledge Management of SAP America, Inc.

About the Contributors

Prior to joining SAP in 2003, Ms. Loisel held global leadership positions with PeopleSoft, a human resource management services provider. She also held sales, marketing, and alliances roles with CODA Ltd., of the United Kingdom, Sterling Commerce, and CompuServe.

Ms. Loisel received a bachelor's of business administration degree from the University of Notre Dame.

Clive Mather is the former President and CEO of Shell Canada.

Mr. Mather's career at Shell spanned thirty-five years and encompassed all of its major businesses, including assignments in Brunei, Gabon, South Africa, the Netherlands, and the United Kingdom. He was appointed President and CEO of Shell Canada in August 2004, a position he held until retiring in June 2007.

Prior to this position, Mr. Mather was Chairman of Shell U.K. and Head of Global Learning in Shell International. He also held numerous positions at the senior management level, with group responsibility for information technology, leadership development, contract and procurement, e-business, and international affairs.

An advocate of leadership and corporate social responsibility issues, Mr. Mather has held many public appointments in the United Kingdom, including Commissioner for the Equal

About the Contributors

Opportunities Commission and Chairman of the U.K. Government/Industry CSR Academy.

Mr. Mather is Chairman of the Shell Pensions Trust Ltd. and also serves on the Royal Anniversary Trust, the Council of The Garden Tomb (Jerusalem) Association, and the Advisory Board of the Relationships Foundation.

Blythe McGarvie is the CEO and Founder of Leadership for International Finance (LIF), a private consulting firm offering a global perspective for clients to achieve profitable growth and providing leadership seminars for corporate and academic groups.

Prior to founding LIF, Ms. McGarvie was based in Paris as the Executive Vice President and Chief Financial Officer of BIC Group, one of the world's leading manufacturers of convenient disposable products. Previously, she served as Senior Vice President and CFO of Hannaford Bros. Co., a *Fortune* 500 supermarket retailer that was acquired by the DelHaize Group in 1999.

Before joining Hannaford, she was Chief Administrative Officer—Pacific Rim, Sara Lee Corporation. In that capacity, she was responsible for the finance, strategy, information systems, and human resources functions for the personal product business in Asia, Australia, and South America, where she grew the division from $124 million to $600 million in sales over a three-year period ending in 1994.

About the Contributors

Ms. McGarvie is a certified public accountant and earned an MBA degree from Kellogg Graduate School of Management at Northwestern University. She received the Kellogg Graduate School of Management Schaffner Award, presented to an alumnus(a) who is preeminent in his or her field and who provided outstanding service to Kellogg. In 2003, she was appointed as Senior Fellow of The Kellogg Innovation Network.

Ms. McGarvie currently serves on the boards of Accenture, Pepsi Bottling Group, St. Paul Travelers, and Wawa.

Sir Michael Rake is Chairman of BT Group, one of the world's leading providers of communications solutions and services. He is Chairman of the U.K. Commission for Employment and Skills, as well as a Director of Barclays plc, the McGraw-Hill Companies, and the Financial Reporting Council. He is also Chairman of the Guidelines Monitoring Committee, a private equity oversight group. From May 2002 to September 2007, Sir Michael was Chairman of KPMG International. Before that appointment, he was Chairman of KPMG in Europe and Senior Partner of KPMG in the United Kingdom.

He joined KPMG in 1974 and worked in Continental Europe before transferring to the Middle East to run the practice for three years in 1986. He transferred to London in 1989, became a member of the U.K. Board in 1991, and had a number of leadership roles in the United Kingdom before being elected U.K. Senior Partner in 1998.

Sir Michael is also a Vice President of the RNIB (Royal National Institute of Blind People) and a member of the Board of the TransAtlantic Business Dialogue, the CBI International Advisory Board, the Chartered Management Institute, the Department of Trade and Industry's U.S./U.K. Regulatory Taskforce, the Advisory Council for Business for New Europe, the Ethnic Minority Employment Taskforce, the School of Oriental and African Studies Advisory Board, the Advisory Board of the Judge Institute at the University of Cambridge, and the Global Advisory Board of the Oxford University Centre for Corporate Reputation. He is a Senior Adviser for Chatham House and an Association Member of BUPA.

Gerry Roche is the Senior Chairman of the executive search firm Heidrick & Struggles.

In his early career, Mr. Roche was an Account Executive for the American Broadcasting Company; a Sales Manager, Product Manager, and Marketing Director for Mobil Oil Company's plastics subsidiary, Kordite Corporation; and a management trainee at AT&T.

Mr. Roche joined Heidrick & Struggles in 1964, where he has remained for more than forty years. He became Senior Vice President and Eastern Manager in 1973. Four years later, he became Executive Vice President, responsible for all domestic operations. A year later, Mr. Roche became President and CEO. In 1981, he moved into the Chairman's role, permitting him more time to conduct high-level international search work. Thirteen years later, Mr. Roche cofounded Heidrick & Struggles' Office of the Chairman with John Thompson. During his time at the firm, Mr. Roche has conducted CEO searches for various companies, including 3M, IBM, The GAP, PricewaterhouseCoopers, and Chubb Corporation.

In addition, he is on the boards of the Community Anti-Drug Coalitions of America.

Dame Anita Roddick, who passed away in September 2007, originally trained as a teacher. She then worked for the United Nations in Geneva before running a restaurant and hotel in Littlehampton, Sussex.

She started The Body Shop in Brighton in 1976 to create a livelihood for herself and her two daughters while her husband was trekking across the Americas. She had no training or experience, but economic necessity—combined with the colorful experiences she had gained from her various travels—saw the creation of a successful business dedicated to the pursuit of social and environmental change. The Body Shop went public in 1984. It has grown from one store in England to a multinational company with nearly two thousand stores in fifty countries.

About the Contributors

Anita Roddick became a Dame in July 2003 for services to retailing, the environment, and charity.

Truett Tate is the Group Executive Director of Lloyds TSB, a U.K.-based financial services group that provides a wide range of banking and financial services to personal and corporate customers.

Prior to joining Lloyds, he served with the international financial conglomerate Citigroup from 1972 to 1999, where he held a number of senior and general management appointments in the United States, South America, Asia, and Europe. He was President and CEO of eCharge Corporation, a global payments company, from 1999 to 2001 and was Cofounder and Vice Chairman of Chase Cost Management, a boutique firm that provides expense-reduction services, from 1996 to 2003.

Mr. Tate joined the Lloyds group in 2003 as Managing Director, Corporate Banking, before being appointed to the board as an Executive Director in 2004.

Mr. Tate also serves as a Director of BritishAmerican Business, a transatlantic organization dedicated to helping its members build their international business. He is a member of the fund-raising board of the National Society for the Prevention of Cruelty to Children.

Ying Yeh is the Chairman and President, North Asia Region; President, Business Development,

About the Contributors

Asia Pacific Region; and Vice President for the imaging innovator Eastman Kodak Company.

Ms. Yeh joined Eastman Kodak in January 1997 as General Manager for External Affairs and Vice President of the Greater China Region. She was responsible for managing government affairs and public relations for Eastman Kodak's Greater China Region, which includes China, Hong Kong, and Taiwan. She was one of the three members of the core negotiating team that successfully secured approval for Kodak's unprecedented US$1.2 billion project to build China's modern sensitizing industry.

Ms. Yeh's responsibilities were expanded in March 1999, when she became General Manager—External Affairs and Vice President— Greater Asia Region. In January 2001, Ms. Yeh was also appointed as Vice Chairman—China to reflect her pivotal role in the execution of Kodak's growth strategy in China, Hong Kong, and Taiwan. In May 2002, the Board of Directors of Eastman Kodak Company elected Ms. Yeh a Vice President of the company.

In April 2004, Ms. Yeh became Chairman—Greater China Region, and in October 2005, she became Chairman and President—North Asia Region. Since she assumed her current role in December 2007, she has been responsible for developing new business opportunities for the company in the region.

She is Chairman of Kodak (China) Company Ltd., Kodak (China) Investment Company Ltd.,

About the Contributors

Kodak (Wuxi) Company Ltd., Kodak (Shanghai) International Trading Company Ltd., and Kodak (Guangzhou) Technology Service Company Ltd.

Prior to joining Kodak, Ms. Yeh had a distinguished career in the U.S. Foreign Service. Ms. Yeh joined the Foreign Service in 1970, following a career in Taiwan and Japan as a radio and television journalist, and served as a Political Officer with the U.S. Embassy in Burma and later with the U.S. Consulate General in Hong Kong.

⊰ ACKNOWLEDGMENTS ⊱

First and foremost, a heartfelt thanks goes to all of the executives who have candidly shared their hard-won experience and battle-tested insights for the *Lessons Learned* series.

We would also like to thank Professor David Grayson and the Doughty Centre for Corporate Responsibility (www.doughtycentre.info) at Cranfield University School of Management for permission to use some of the lessons we produced in partnership.

Angelia Herrin at Harvard Business Publishing consistently offered unwavering support, good humor, and counsel from the inception of this ambitious project.

Brian Surette and David Goehring provided invaluable editorial direction, perspective, and encouragement, particularly for this second series. Many thanks to the entire HBP team of designers, copy editors, and marketing professionals who helped bring this series to life.

Much appreciation goes to Jennifer Lynn and Christopher Benoît for research and diligent attention to detail, and to Roberto de Vicq de Cumptich for his imaginative cover designs.

Finally, thanks to James MacKinnon and the entire 50 Lessons team for their time, effort, and steadfast support of this project.